LOAD LIFTERS

LOAD LIFTERS

Derricks, Cranes, and Helicopters

Hope Irvin Marston
Illustrated with photographs

DODD, MEAD & COMPANY
New York

The photographs in this book are used by permission and through the courtesy of: AeroLift, Inc., 61; Alimak, Inc., 42, 53; Barko Hydraulics, Inc., 37; Bromma, Inc., 50; Burro Crane, Inc., 36; Clyde-AMCA International Corporation, 24; Columbia Helicopters, Inc., 57, 58, 59; Crane Carrier Company, 39; Crane Manufacturing and Service Corp., 47, 49; Gorbel, Inc., 28; Iowa Mold Tooling Co., Inc., 30, 31, 33; Kockums AB, 55; Manitowoc Engineering Co., 34, 41, 44, 45; Arthur Marston, 18; Lee C. Moore Corp., 20, 21; Northwest Engineering Company, 35; Oshkosh Truck Corporation, 32; Paceco, Inc., 9, 51, 52; Pacific Hoist, 19; Sikorsky Aircraft, 6, 56; Spanco, Inc., 29; Tennessee Valley Authority, 48; Whiting Corporation, 46. Drawings by Maria Magdalena Brown, 10, 11, 12, 13, 14, 16, 23, 25, 27, 62.

Published by Dodd, Mead & Company, Inc., 71 Fifth Avenue, New York, N.Y. 10003
Printed in Singapore by Tien Wah Press

1   2   3   4   5   6   7   8   9   10

Library of Congress Cataloging-in-Publication Data
Marston, Hope Irvin.
Load lifters.
Includes index.
Summary: Introduces hoists, derricks, cranes, helicopters and other machines that lift heavy loads.
1. Hoisting machinery—Juvenile literature.   2. Cranes, derricks, etc.—Juvenile literature.   3. Helicopters—Juvenile literature.   [1. Hoisting machinery.   2. Cranes, derricks, etc.]   I. Title.
TJ1363.M284   1988   621.8′62   87-27195
ISBN 0-396-09226-8

For Shirley and Lyman

I wish to thank the following for their assistance in the preparation of this book:

John W. Born, Chief Engineer, Lee C. Moore Corp.

John E. Derbyshire, U.S. Army Corps of Engineers

Steve Khail, Advertising Manager, Manitowoc Engineering Company

Mike Larson, Literature Development and Distribution Supervisor, Manitowoc Engineering Company

Dave Peck, Chief Engineer, Manitowoc Engineering Company

Jack Perry, U.S. Army Corps of Engineers

Pete Runquist, Director, Duluth Operations, Clyde-AMCA International

I am also indebted to the many manufacturers who generously supplied the photographs for this book.

Our muscles enable us to lift objects with ease. Yet sometimes what must be lifted is too heavy for them. Then we need powerful load lifters—hoists, derricks, cranes, or helicopters to help us.

We see these big machines at oil wells and at construction sites. But loads must also be lifted in other places. A wrecker pulls a big truck back onto the highway after it loses control on an icy pavement. Lift cranes clean up the mess when two locomotives collide. Huge floating cranes right a capsized ferry. A skycrane moves a home to its new location.

Cranes are custom-built for special jobs. Tall tower cranes are used at construction sites. Huge gantry-mounted cranes (like the one opposite) load heavy containers and bulky materials onto ships. Powerful industrial cranes move tons of materials in warehouses, foundaries, mills, and machine shops.

Specially designed cranes lift logs or stacked lumber for the forest industry. Rake cranes move piles of chips or sawdust. Whether you are moving a house or stacking containers on a ship, load lifters can do the job with the least amount of waste, expense, and effort.

Long ago cavemen used poles and vines to move heavy loads. Hunters tied their game to a pole with a vine and carried it between them—just as these children are carrying their fish.

Then they discovered that they could lift their game up by putting the vine over a tree branch and pulling downward—like drawing water from a well. That was much easier.

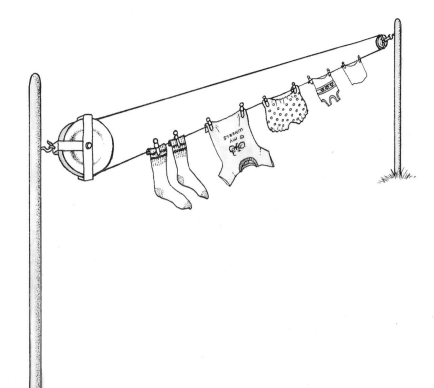

Modern lifting machines use ropes or steel cable. They are powered by gasoline, diesel fuel, or electricity. Pulleys and movable booms (long poles extending upward at an angle) make the work easier.

Pulleys (like the one for the well) change the direction of the pull on a rope. That means you can lift something up by pulling down. You use pulleys when you raise the flag or hang out laundry.

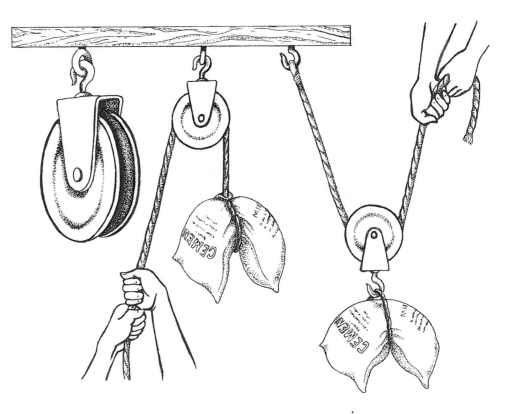

A pulley has a grooved wheel called a *sheave* which keeps the rope in place. At left is what it looks like without the rope. The center drawing is a fixed (fastened) pulley like the one on a flag pole. On the right is a movable pulley that you will find on a hoist.

If you use a movable pulley and fasten one end of the rope to a limb, the limb will support one-half the load. You lift the other half.

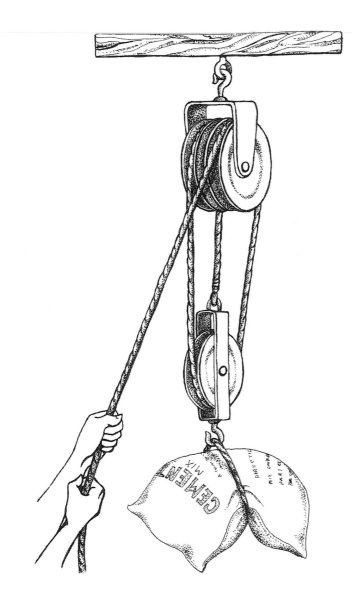

Pulleys were once carved from blocks of wood. Today they are still called *blocks*. A combination of fixed and movable pulleys is called a *hoist*, or a *block and tackle*. The tackle is the rope or cable. One block is usually fastened to an overhead support. The movable block is attached to the load.

It's easier to pull down on a rope that has been led over a fixed pulley. Still, a 78-pound pull is needed to lift a 78-pound sheepdog. If you use a movable pulley with the rope fastened overhead, the rope will support one-half the weight (39 pounds), and you only have to pull one-half the weight. If you pass the rope through three pulleys, you only need to lift one-third the weight of the dog, or 26 pounds. To lift the 78-pound dog one foot, using the three pulleys, a boy must pull three feet of rope. But that's easier than lifting 78 pounds one foot. (See next page.)

The block-and-tackle hoisting arrangement of three pulleys gives the boy a *mechanical advantage*. Mechanical advantage is the relation of the pull or effort to the load. When a 26-pound effort lifts a 78-pound load, the pulleys provide a mechanical advantage of three —which is the same as the number of ropes supporting the load. Mechanical advantage can be increased by using more pulleys and ropes or cables. Nearly every crane system uses the block-and-tackle principle.

It takes a lot of rope or cable to raise a heavy load, so a *winch* is used. A winch is a reel or steel drum around which the rope or cable winds as the block and tackle lifts the load. The drum is attached to a strong steel shaft which is turned by an engine or motor. Here's a close-up of the winch on a wrecker.

A block and tackle like the one shown here usually
hangs above the load that is to be lifted. Derricks, masts,
and cranes have giant blocks and tackles.

Derricks and masts can only move loads within reach of their movable booms. They have rigging—ropes, pulleys, and winches—and an engine for power. In oil drilling operations, they hold the equipment in place that is used to dig (bore) the well. They also raise, lower, and support the heavy steel pipe in the well bore (hole). They can be used in construction, shipbuilding, and mining.

This mast operates in a Texas oil field.

Derricks are assembled in an upright position. Masts are built in a horizontal position on the ground and then raised.

This derrick drills for oil at an offshore drilling site.

A guy derrick has a vertical pole, also called a mast, held up by strong steel guy wires. These wires are anchored deep in the ground or to a strong support to keep the derrick upright. On top of the mast the guy wires are fastened to a steel plate that is fitted over a heavy pin. This allows the mast to turn without twisting the wires. The bottom of the mast is set on heavy wood or steel girders. The boom is attached to the mast, so that the boom and the mast rotate together. The mast is turned by a large bull wheel.

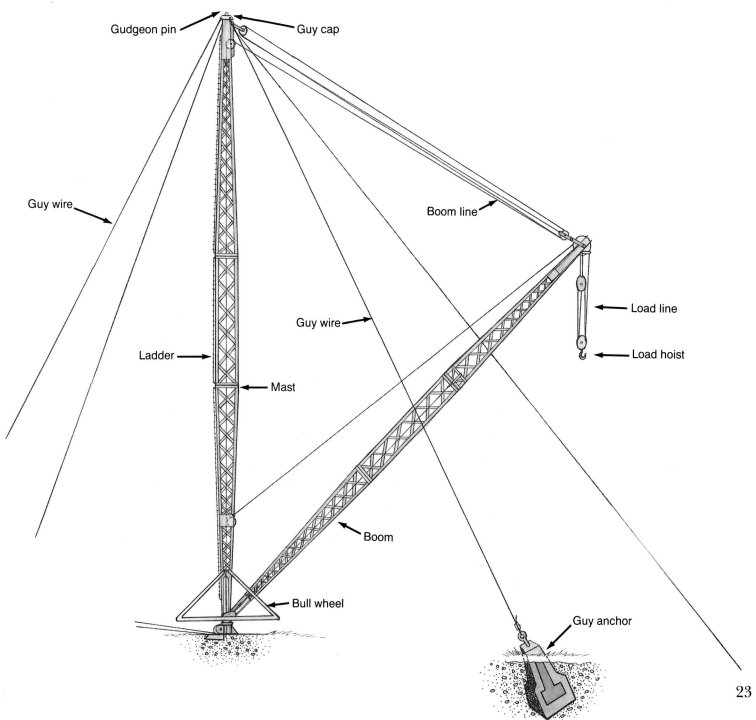

Gudgeon pin

Guy cap

Guy wire

Boom line

Load line

Load hoist

Guy wire

Ladder

Mast

Boom

Bull wheel

Guy anchor

23

A stiff-legged derrick is fixed to a frame. Its girders support a single short mast. It can be equipped with a bucket or a hook, depending on what kind of load it will be lifting.

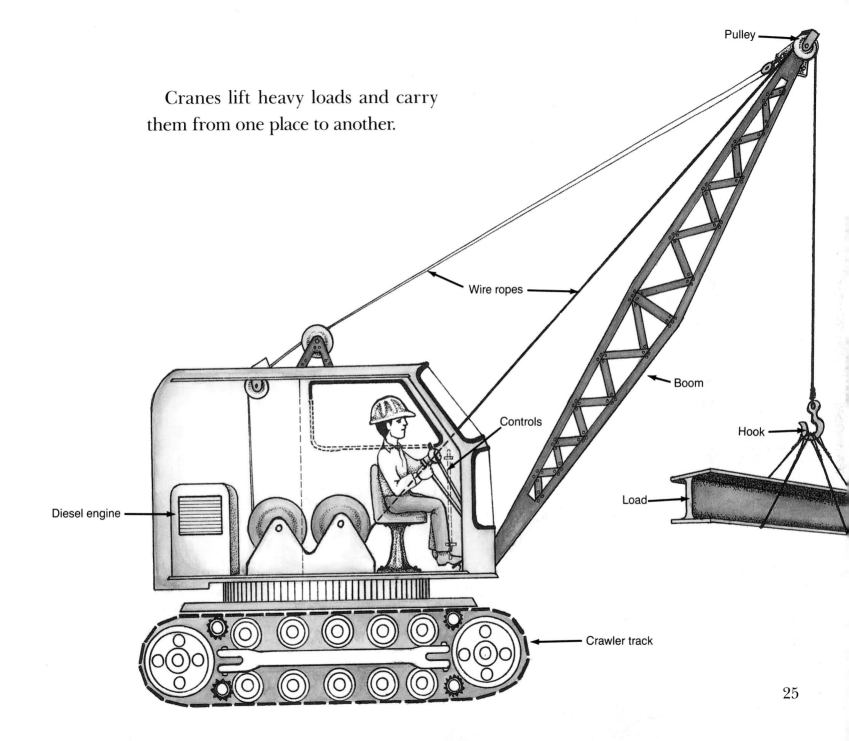

Cranes lift heavy loads and carry them from one place to another.

Pulley

Wire ropes

Boom

Controls

Hook

Load

Diesel engine

Crawler track

25

Cranes can be fitted with lifting attachments. Webs, nets, ropes, or cables attached to the hook will handle boxes or bags. A dragline winches back bucketloads of ore, gravel, or earth. It can also dig an underwater channel.

A crane can be fitted with different kinds of attachments. You dig with a *clamshell bucket,* or lift metal with an *electromagnet.* You clean out a catch basin with a *spring bucket,* or pick up hay, lumber, or bales of scrap with a *tined grapple.*

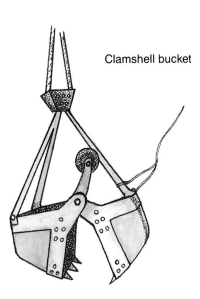

Clamshell bucket

Electromagnet

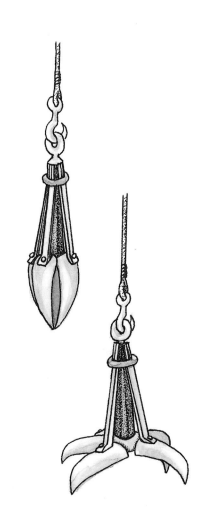

Tined grapple

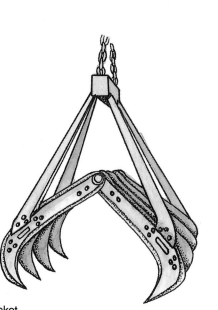

Spring bucket

27

The jib crane, also called a hammerhead crane, has a rotating boom, called a jib, that is attached to a mast. The jib moves in a circle to spot (place) the load exactly where it is wanted. The crane can be mounted to a column or a wall, like this one.

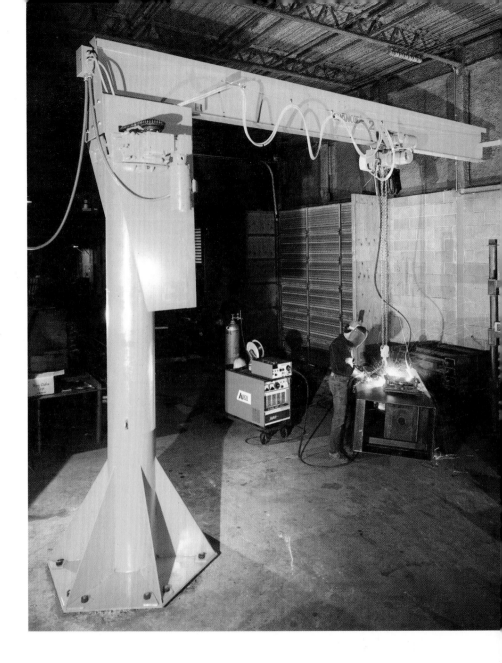

A pillar crane is a jib crane which supports itself. The jib is attached to the pillar. It moves up and down, as well as from side to side.

The cranes you see most often are mobile cranes. They can move about the workplace to where they are needed. Small ones are mounted on trucks. They handle things like equipment to change a five-ton tire (above) or farm equipment (opposite).

This mobile crane picks up cinder blocks.

A hydraulic, telescoping, truck-mounted crane handles a large portable electric welder.

Crawler cranes are mounted on tracks like a Caterpillar tractor. They have to be carried to the workplace. Cranes like these with no jibs are called lift cranes.

This lift crane uses a sling to unload logs.

Some mobile cranes operate on railroad tracks. This one is a magnet crane. It moves tie plates, rail joints, and scrap metal.

The rough terrain carrier has unusually large wheels to help it operate on uneven ground without gouging or sinking.

Crane carriers are heavy-duty trucks built with special creeping gears. They have as many as 33 forward gears to help them operate on the highway as well as on the job. The creeping gears provide extra power to move the heavy equipment slowly over rough terrain. Brakes on crane carriers are extra strong.

Carriers in the United States can be 13 feet wide. They must get special permission to travel on highways. This crane carrier has "telescoped down" a 96-foot well-servicing derrick.

Tower cranes look like tall, latticed towers with latticed booms which can be raised or lowered. They are used in construction work in areas where the crane must be placed close to a building and still be able to raise loads over or beyond the building.

It takes a lot of planning to install a tower crane at a jobsite. It is costly to move its parts, to erect it, and then take it down. Yet for some jobs it is the most economical way to get the work done. Many contractors rent tower cranes rather than buying them.

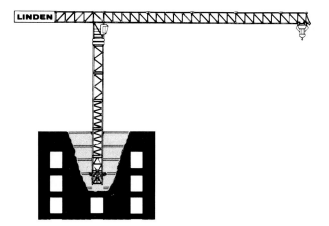

A climbing tower crane can be erected within a building under construction. It is raised through the floors as work progresses (see diagram).

The climbing tower crane can be operated by remote control.

A crane can lift much more weight if you mount the boom, body, and the cab on a boom carrier with large high-capacity rollers. The rollers allow the boom to rotate in a large circle. RINGER and Whirley are trade names for revolving cranes.

Revolving cranes are quite stable. However, extremely heavy loads may require a counterweight to keep them from tipping. They can be mounted on tops of buildings or gantries (bridgelike frames), on barges, in highly congested areas, or on rough, sloping terrain.

Revolving cranes are used in industrial construction, power plant work, pile driving, jetty construction, and offshore petroleum work.

This crane has a 140-foot boom and a 130-foot mast. It is lifting a nuclear pressure vessel from a barge. The total weight is 415 tons. The counterweight weighs 420 tons.

This crane was built to handle large, bulky containers as gently as fine china.

An overhead crane, also called a bridge crane, rides on a runway or a pair of tracks above the work floor. It has a trolley-mounted hoisting system and a bridge spanning the tracks. It is used chiefly in industry.

A gantry crane is an overhead traveling crane mounted on legs which ride on rails. This double-leg gantry crane has a magnet that handles rails and plates in a railroad yard.

When one end of the bridge of a crane is on legs and the other on a runway beam, the machine is called a semigantry crane. This 270-ton crane hoists the gates that close off the flow of water through a dam.

This grapple crane moves 5,000 tons of sugar cane daily at the refinery. It has an underslung cab for the operator on the left.

Straddle cranes straddle the load they carry. Both gantry and semigantry cranes are really straddle cranes. So are stacker cranes. Straddle cranes can lift from 25,000 to 500,000 pounds. This one is mounted on pneumatic tires.

The stacker crane opposite is built to stack containers at dockside prior to loading a ship.

The trolley travels between the legs of this ship-to-shore crane that handles containers.

The elevator on this container crane carries the operators to their stations. The time saved speeds up operations.

The world's largest crane, the Kockums' goliath crane in Sweden, weighs 7,200 tons. It is 459 feet tall and can lift 1,400 tons. Each leg runs on 48 wheels on tracks that are 2,329 feet long and 571 feet wide. The crane and its tracks cover an area which includes the building dock, the assembly shed, and the storage shed. The letters in the name "Kockums" on the sides of the beams are more than 39 feet high.

The crane is used to move the steel plate from the plate yard to the hull of a ship. Here it is lifting the bow section of a supertanker under construction.

Heavy loads need to be lifted in areas where you can't take derricks or cranes. Companies such as Boeing Vertol and Sikorsky build helicopters that work like "flying trucks." This Super Stallion can lift more than 16 tons.

Columbia Helicopters uses its Boeing Vertol 107 to harvest southern yellow pine...

...and to move logs from the cutting area to the log landing.

This helicopter transports pipe for
a paint shop in Missouri.

The Cyclo-Crane is a 178-foot helium-filled, experimental winged airship. It moves like a helicopter, but flies like an airplane. The wings are parallel to the horizontal structure when the airship is hovering. To go from hover to flight, the center-body spins. The blades swivel and the propellers tilt at a 90° angle. Two engines, on opposite wings, push the center-body into a counterclockwise whirl. When the Cyclo-Crane reaches maximum speed, which is about 40 mph, it stops whirling and flies like a plane.

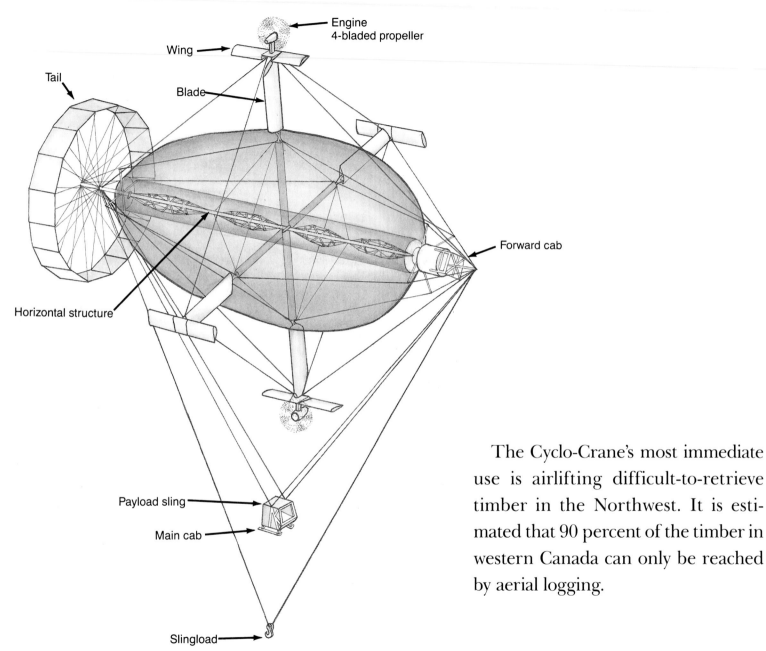

Engine
4-bladed propeller

Wing

Tail

Blade

Forward cab

Horizontal structure

Payload sling

Main cab

Slingload

The Cyclo-Crane's most immediate use is airlifting difficult-to-retrieve timber in the Northwest. It is estimated that 90 percent of the timber in western Canada can only be reached by aerial logging.

Glossary

AERIAL LOGGING—Going into an area by plane or helicopter to cut trees and remove the logs

BOOM—A long pole extending upward or outward from the mast of a derrick

BOOM CARRIER—A machine built for carrying revolving cranes

BULL WHEEL—A wheel at the bottom of a derrick that turns the mast

CABLE—A strong rope, wire, or chain

COUNTERWEIGHT—A weight used to keep a crane from tipping when it is carrying a heavy load

CRANE—A machine for lifting and carrying heavy objects; often mounted on a truck

DERRICK—A lifting machine that usually remains in one place

DRAGLINE—A line used for dragging buckets of earth or gravel; a line used to sweep the bottom of a body of water with a grappling hook, a dragnet, or a dredge

GANTRY—A bridgelike frame over which a traveling crane moves

GIRDER—A strong, horizontal beam used as a main support

GUY WIRES—Steel wires that support a derrick

HOIST—A piece of equipment used for lifting

JIB—The "arm" of a crane

LATTICE—A framework of crossed metal strips

MAST—A vertical pole; also a derrick that is assembled on the ground and then raised

MECHANICAL ADVANTAGE—The relationship between the weight of a load and how much effort it takes to lift it

PULLY—A wheel with a grooved rim through which a rope or chain is pulled to lift a load

REMOTE CONTROL—Control by radioed instruction

RIGGING—The ropes, pulleys, and winches used to control a lifting machine

TELESCOPE—To slide round sections inside one another to make a piece of equipment shorter for transporting

TROLLEY—A cage or basket with wheels that travels on an overhead track

Index